CATS HOME ALONE

First published as *Katze Allein zu Haus*
German edition © 2019 by Eugen Ulmer KG, Stuttgart, Germany

Translation from German: Rae Walter, in association with First Edition
Translations Ltd, Cambridge, UK © Heike Grotegut 2020

Heike Grotegut has asserted her right to be identified as the author
of this work.

English language edition first published in October 2020

British Library Cataloguing in Publication Data
A catalogue record for this book is available from the British Library.

ISBN 978 1 78521 735 7

Library of Congress catalog card no. 2020941628

Published by JH Haynes & Co. Ltd,
Sparkford, Yeovil, Somerset BA22 7JJ, UK
Tel: 01963 440635
Int. tel: +44 1963 440635
Website: www.haynes.com

Haynes North America Inc.
859 Lawrence Drive, Newbury Park,California 91320, USA

Printed and bound in Malaysia

While every effort is taken to ensure the accuracy of the information given in
this book, no liability can be accepted by the author or publishers for any loss,
damage or injury caused by errors in, or omissions from the information given.

CATS HOME ALONE

ALL YOU NEED TO KNOW IN ONE CONCISE MANUAL

Heike Grotegut

Contents

The house of the rising fun

Bye-bye boredom: intriguing toys, interesting views, cosy resting places and a living space suited to cats' tastes will guarantee fun and comfort for our furry friends.

Home alone

Do you sometimes wonder what your cats are doing when they're alone in the house all day? Do they sit waiting by the window for hours, longing for you to come home and drowning in a sea of boredom? Do they turn the house upside down just for something to do? Or do they get hungry and start climbing up the walls?

And what about you? Are you plagued by a guilty conscience when you're working or travelling and you think about your furry friend? Can you not get home quickly enough to see whether all's well with your pussycat? Are you maybe even stressed by the thought that you have to go out again in the evening? If you are familiar with any of these situations, this book may help to make your guilty conscience disappear and give you a better understanding of your pet.

Adieu tristesse

While we're out of the house, our cats are sitting at home – and often there's not a lot going on. In that situation, a creature as intelligent as a cat can easily go stir-crazy. Some cats get creative about how to escape boredom. Objects on shelves that were previously of no interest are suddenly transformed into exciting prey when nudged with a paw. Or perhaps the kitchen roll has to be shredded, because it's eager to start a fight. The curtain offers a tempting glimpse of breathtaking climbs, possibly with an exciting unknown view of the surroundings. Toilet paper must be properly unrolled; after all, it's enticing as a wonderfully cosy nest that is perfect for hiding in.

← An adventure playground for cats: soft, cosy and exciting – though to us it's just toilet paper.

Some cats stuff themselves with food out of boredom and gradually become fatter and fatter, which may have serious consequences for their physical and mental health. Others feel so stressed out by long periods of solitude that they may either lick themselves bald or become aggressive. Boredom and loneliness may also lead to scent marking, undesirable scratching, attention-seeking behaviour or even depression.

It doesn't have to be like this. It's so easy to prevent boredom from occurring in the first place. Many of the ideas presented here can be put into practice swiftly and simply, using things that are mostly to be found in the home or are destined for charity collections or the dustbin.

Everybody's different – and of course that also applies to our favourite pets – so not all of the ideas suggested here will go down equally well with every cat. Let the suggestions inspire you and try out a few different ones. Discover what works best together with your furry friend.

I hope you and your cat will have a lot of fun experimenting and exploring while playing and relaxing together.

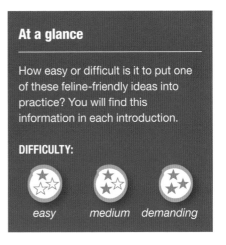

At a glance

How easy or difficult is it to put one of these feline-friendly ideas into practice? You will find this information in each introduction.

DIFFICULTY:

easy   medium   demanding

House
beautiful

Welcome to dreamland

The expression '*dolce far niente*' – sweet idleness – must surely have come into existence at the sight of a sleeping cat: almost nothing is more appealing. How lovely that our furry friends also like to have a siesta...

Cats sleep a lot. In fact, they spend up to two-thirds of the day in intensive idleness. They relax happily and appreciatively, sometimes in acrobatic positions and in uncomfortable-looking places that would make a fakir go green with envy. Sleeping positions have much to do with individual preferences. For instance, for many cats, the world appears upside down, simply because they love to sleep lying on their backs. Their famous stubbornness also shows itself in their choice of resting place; an empty pizza box often seems more attractive than an expensive cat bed.

Just take it easy

Cats are hunters and hunting is an occupation that involves lying in wait, stalking, making a lightning-fast pounce on the prey, jumping and climbing. They practise this activity all the time and everywhere, even when they are 'only' pursuing a toy or playing a game within their own four walls. Such activity requires extreme concentration, the adrenalin level shoots up and the body uses a lot of energy – even during a brief stalk.

The best way of recharging the batteries is clearly taking a short nap. This is not only an opportunity for the cat to recover lost energy, but it also enables the cat to process what it has experienced, so it feels stronger after its sleep and ready for a new bout of activity.

A rumbling tummy may make some cats react aggressively; admonitory smacks with paws and claws tell the person who feeds them that a meal is needed urgently. After eating, our four-legged housemates like to indulge in the comfort of an after-dinner nap.

Every cat has its own individual needs for sleep, determined by factors such as age, health, time of year and current living conditions. A cat in a clean indoor environment without anything special to do sleeps more than one that goes hunting outdoors. Young kittens sleep a lot – the exciting adventures, amusing games and all their new knowledge must be processed in the arms of Morpheus. During their sleep, kittens recharge their batteries, ready for further fascinating discoveries. Older cats no longer have to prove themselves by adventuring and really appreciate a long snooze in a warm, cosy place. Be kind and let sleeping cats lie. Waking them can really stress them out; after all, who enjoys being rudely awakened?

Ideal places for cats

Our furry friends are happiest if they can spend dull days and wet, cold hours in comfortable places near radiators, with a cosy blanket or on a soft cushion. If it's hot outside, cooler places are in great demand; then they like to lie where there's a gentle breeze or on cool tiles. They generally sleep more in winter than on warm summer days.

The choice of resting place is influenced by the time of day as well as by the seasons. In the morning, your cats will certainly sleep in a different place from where they slept at night. Generally speaking, they prefer soft, dry, warm places. They particularly like containers that are only just big enough for their body to squeeze into. The more unsafe an animal feels, the more protection it will

⬇ Cats love to sleep in boxes that are only slightly larger than they are, as it makes them feel safe.

seek in which to take a break. It's no wonder that cats are truly, madly, deeply in love with cardboard boxes.

Some cats can only completely relax in places that are extremely well hidden from view, such as in a box under a bed. Many love to observe things from beneath a protected covering, so they are tempted either by a place under the sofa or the

⬇ Amazing fact: cats recover their energy during sleep, yet they don't miss much because they remain alert.

table or by a high position that offers a perfect all-round view of the room, from which every minute change can be registered. Cats hunt by lying in wait and prowling. That is why intense observation of their surroundings is so important for them; they never know where and when the next potential prey will appear. Of course, the humans who feed them and groom them are just as keenly observed and studied.

As a rule, one cat's favourite retreat is respected by others and they leave one

another in peace. However, in the event of any take-over attempt, this little piece of paradise will likely be fiercely defended.

Time Lord

Cats do not go through life without a plan; like many other animals, they have a definite sense of time. They do things according to a fixed timetable that covers checking their territory, stalking, snoozing, mealtimes and playtimes. Such polished time management offers a number of advantages, including making the best joint use of slender resources. Cats who share the same paths through their territory take care to use them at different times so that they don't get in each other's way.

Cats are creatures of the twilight hours, being most active in the early dawn and at dusk. That is when their prey is busy outside, so they naturally make good use of these parts of the day. In addition to their own daily rhythm, cats memorise the regular habits of their human companions and adjust their lives accordingly. The day and a large part of the night are not good times for hunting anyway, so they are very sensibly used for relaxing snoozes. It's handy that this mostly suits our schedules perfectly. During the day, we're working or doing things outside the house, and at night we're sleeping. The absence of humans is exploited for a long, relaxing siesta. This adaptation and merging of two timetables shows how intelligent cats are. When you come home tired and hungry, they are fresh and relaxed and wanting to be entertained. The world is just not fair. When you are there, they feel the time is ripe for playing and having adventures together and, of course, for a cuddle. What could be nicer?

Cometh the hour, cometh sleep

There are various alternating stages of sleep. In the 15- to 30-minute phase of light sleep, cats may momentarily wake and react. This is reflected in the position of their bodies: their ears remain pricked, often one eye is half open and in addition they respond directly to ambient noises – a relic of their life in the wild, where it's better to be alert all the time and not miss the next prey. In the five- to eight-minute deep-sleep phase, the body functions in stand-by mode; the muscles are relaxed, the ears are no longer pricked, a paw may twitch occasionally and the brain remains active. The eyes move quickly behind the closed lids, which gives this phase the name Rapid Eye Movement (REM). Scientists assume that cats dream during this phase. Anyone who has ever watched their cat at this time will have no doubt about it.

The lion's den

Feral cats don't live in packs. In the event of danger, they have to reach safety and manage completely on their own, with no help when recovering from injuries. In this kind of world, foresight is better than hindsight. So these animals thoroughly inspect all possible means of flight and places of shelter in their surroundings, and they have the ability to find a hiding place (almost) anywhere. When touring their home territory, your cats will also certainly scout out holes, pipes, large crevices and so on. They especially like to disappear into cardboard boxes, paper bags, sports bags or cupboards – which stems from a natural tendency cats have to hide in crevices. These 'dens' promise shelter and security.

Tips and tricks

Whether you want to provide your cat with interesting entertainment when they're left alone, a chill-out zone, or spaces in which they can roam in the indoor territory, you need to bear in mind a few safety rules to keep them from harm.

Unlimited freedom?

Cats demarcate their territory. They are familiar with this and expect others to do the same. Our furry housemates need boundaries – totally unlimited freedom is absolutely not what they expect. However, it is typical cat behaviour to occasionally test out taboos, investigate existing frameworks and rebel against restrictions. These transgressions are a deliberate provocation. If the opposition refuses to give up, the matter is usually quickly sorted out.

For example, not every room has to be permanently accessible – assuming, of course, that there is sufficient space. After all, their outdoor territory is also restricted, by other cats or animals or by buildings. A closed door inevitably leads to our little friends – out of sheer curiosity – attempting to work out how to turn or push down handles and access all areas. They inspect and lie in wait, which is a very simple way of briefly breaking through the everyday monotony every now and then.

Not without my cat

The earliest archaeological find of a cat was made in a 9,500-year-old grave in Cyprus, located less than 40cm (8in) away from the body of a young man. Both were ritually laid out facing the west. This is puzzling since at this time there were no domestic cats in Cyprus.

Safe home, happy alone

'Curiosity killed the cat.' This traditional saying refers to cats' boundless compulsion to investigate all the hiding places, spaces and objects in their surroundings and preferably crawl into them in order to examine everything in more detail. If you share your life with cats, you just have to be prepared for their sudden appearance in the strangest places. No hiding place is too bizarre, no bag too small. Newspapers or blankets make good hideouts and cardboard boxes are the classic refuge. Be prepared for anything; nothing is impossible. Unfortunately, not all risks are obvious. There are some things you need to pay attention to, to make sure that your pets are safe when playing, dozing or patrolling their territory alone in the home.

Here are a few tips:

- **Windows and doors:** Use doorstops or wedges to secure doors and windows that might slam otherwise shut in a draught. Keep all windows closed during your absence and, if appropriate, secure them with a safety net. Every year, far too many cats are seriously injured by falling from windows and many end up suffering a painful death.
- **Toilets:** Keep the lids closed. Young kittens can drown in the toilet bowl, while adult animals can be poisoned by chemicals in the water.

Plants: Please ensure that no plants or flowers in your home are poisonous to cats. Leaves, flowers, stems, pollen and even the water they are standing in may cause serious poisoning (check the internet for species to avoid).

Vases and pots: Secure pot plants and flower vases in such a way that they can't fall and break. Shards and splinters may injure your pets.

Medicines: Please store medicines safely away from cats. Painkillers containing paracetamol, ibuprofen and/or diclofenac are poisonous to cats, as are contraceptive pills, thyroid

↑ Paper bags make seductive hidey-holes for cats: the perfect place from which to observe their surroundings without immediately being spotted.

hormones, beta-blockers – for instance, for treating heart conditions – ADHD medicines and antidepressants.

Cleaning materials: Store household cleaners out of reach of felines. Concentrated products such as toilet and drain cleaners may cause chemical burns. Pine oil and citrus oil are often used in cleaning products and may cause numerous problems, including organ damage.

■ **De-icers:** These are lethal to cats, so please securely shut away all de-icer containers without exception and wipe up any spilled spray.

■ **Food, alcohol and tobacco:** Many of these items are poisonous to cats, though this does not claim to be a complete list: chives; onions; grapes and raisins; chocolate and cocoa; avocados; cabbage; pulses; stone fruits such as apricots, plums and peaches; raw potatoes; aubergines; tomatoes; macadamia nuts; tobacco; nutmeg; alcohol; coffee and tea; garlic in large quantities. The consumption of raw pork carries the risk of infection with Aujeszky's disease, also known as pseudorabies, which can cause incurable inflammation of the brain or bone marrow. Because cats clean themselves often and thoroughly, many substances can be picked up as they lick their paws or fur.

■ **Ribbons etc.:** Carefully tidy away long threads, rubber bands, cords, balls of wool, gift ties, shoelaces, toy fishing rods with long lines and similar things. Unfortunately, cats find these little 'snakes' very attractive and they can get entangled in them while playing, cut off the circulation to their limbs or strangle themselves. If they swallow them, there is a risk of gastric torsion or intestinal obstruction.

■ **Bags:** Cut through the handles of paper carriers or remove them completely. Cats can get entangled in the loops and injure themselves in their panicky attempts to get free. Plastic bags pose several hazards: there is a risk of suffocation when inquisitive cats inspect these fantastic 'dens', and they are also dangerous if the plastic is pulled apart, bitten or partially swallowed. You should therefore immediately move plastic bags right out of the feline sphere of activity.

■ **Tempting spaces:** It is best to keep the washing machine, clothes drier, dishwasher and cupboards with doors closed at all times. If cats slip into these 'dens' without being noticed and get shut in accidentally, in the worst case they may suffocate. Always check the interior carefully for feline visitors before closing the door.

■ **Tins:** Cats may injure their tongues on the edges of opened tins. In addition, it may happen that a cat sticks its head into the tin and can't manage to free itself – a bitter fate that is frequently suffered by hungry stray cats. You should therefore crush tins as flat as you can, with your foot, before putting them into the recycling.

■ **Small items:** Put small items that can be swallowed – such as needles, drawing pins and the like – away tidily.

■ **Cables and plugs:** Kittens in particular like to nibble cables. Make them safe with appropriate coverings and special child-safety socket covers.

■ **Ironing boards and irons:** Don't leave ironing equipment standing around unattended. Not all ironing boards can withstand a cat jumping on them and they may collapse. This may result in anything from bruising to complex fractures. The same applies to clothes horses.

■ **Waste bins:** Some cats find rubbish extremely interesting and rummage around in it. For obvious reasons, this may pose various dangers, depending on the material. It is best to use inaccessible waste bins with lids.

Fireplaces and chimneys: Take care to block off access to open hearths; otherwise, a curious and athletic cat may end up on the roof.

Balconies: Every year, far too many cats come to grief by falling from a balcony or a wide-open window. Don't rely on their legendary sense of balance or the fact that nothing has happened for years. A bird flying past or a butterfly may instantly trigger the hunting instinct, a loud noise may frighten a cat into losing its balance, or the balcony rail may come away from its mooring when the cat jumps on to it. It is by no means the case that all cats land unharmed on four legs. Only a cat safety net will provide complete security.

Heat sources: It is best to place a pan of water on any hotplate that is still hot, to prevent the cat from coming in contact with it.

Roller blinds and curtains: With indoor roller blinds, please take care that the blinds don't swing around

⬇ Cats love to explore and make use of unexpected places, so make sure they are safe.

freely, so that cats can't get caught in them and be badly injured or even killed. Tie up the cord out of reach. Floaty net curtains are also irresistible to cats, and unfortunately they also pose a risk of strangulation.

⬇ A view from higher up offers a safer observation post – few creatures can follow the cat up here.

- **Necklaces:** Cats can get caught up in hanging necklaces and strangle themselves as they attempt to escape, or else they may suffer nasty injuries to the mouth and paws.
- **Stability:** Cats don't like wobbly cat trees or furniture. In the worst case they tip over with them and get injured.
- **Toy fishing rods:** Get out toys with strings only when you are going to play together; otherwise keep them where your pet can't reach them. Cats may get entangled in them and, if the worst comes to the worst, strangled when playing alone.

Admittedly this looks like a lot. But don't be frightened; the longer you live with your four-legged housemates, the better you will know them and be able to make your home appropriately safe.

Happy at home

You must have experienced this: you've just bought a sensational cat bed and hurry home full of excited anticipation. This new place to relax should make your pets more comfortable and at ease. You arrange the cat bed lovingly in the room and in fact a cat quickly curls up on it. Oh joy! That's exactly how you imagined it. And then? A moment later, the cat aims straight for the cardboard box you just put out for the wastepaper collection. Don't worry, you are not alone in experiencing this. Every cat has peculiar tastes – and this stubbornness is what we love so much about them. Cats seek out their own places to relax and there's no arguing with them about taste.

That said, for all their individuality and stubbornness, there are one or two things that most cats simply can't resist.

Here are a few tips:

- **A good view:** Contemplating the world outside can provide endless hours of entertainment, so a free space by a window is an essential part of a cat's life. Mostly, there's not much going on in the entrance hall that's of interest to cats, so resting places there aren't usually well received.

- **Change of perspective:** Offer cats different levels on which to relax. They like a change of angle occasionally so they can observe the world from different positions. It also expands their living space.

- **Confined spaces:** Position cushions and containers near your sofa, bed or workspace, especially if your cats like to remain within your sight. A blanket or towel on the arm or back of the sofa or on your bed will usually be gratefully accepted and used.

- **Protected view:** Cats love to be able to get inside things – containers are popular for this reason. High sides are attractive, offering a wonderful place to hide on the principle of, 'If I can't see you, you can't see me.'

- **More is more:** The more opportunities there are available for observation and safe retreat, the better. That way, every taste and every situation is provided for. But don't worry, you don't have to furnish your whole home with resting places for cats. All the same, there should be at least two places per cat – although they may well share some areas, and not only at different times.

- **Bewitching scents:** If your cats like catmint or valerian, it may be a good idea to spread a little on a new cushion or cat bed. For many cats it makes attachment to it more attractive.

- **Good view:** A ceiling-high scratching post will greatly enrich a cat's life if it is accessible, stable and in an interesting place. It provides opportunities for climbing, thus increasing living space. In addition, cats gain an overview from a higher vantage point. It's also an advantage in the event of quarrels: the party with the higher perch clearly holds the best cards, even against stronger opponents. A cat tree tucked away in a corner offers a less interesting view and is more rarely accepted.

Test your cats' preferences; after a while, you will certainly get to know what they like best. It's a great feeling when you can be sure that all is well with your cats and that they are well protected when you are absent – especially if they have a great environment and suitable toys (for the subject of safety and toys, see pages 69–70). Goodbye, guilty conscience!

Difficult about-turns

Everyone is familiar with headlines about a cat having to be rescued from a tree. How does such a clever animal come to be in such an awkward position? When squirrels climb downwards, they turn their back feet outwards and slightly backwards. Long curved claws also give them grip. Cats can't do this. They just have to learn how to get back down. It goes against their natural instincts and not being able to see where they are going is unsettling at first. Once they have learned, though, things usually go well – except when fear creates inhibitions.

Come into my wigwam

Cats and confined spaces: this is a great, undying love, which can easily be made to blossom, sometimes by amazingly simple means.

Let's be honest – the vast majority of us cat lovers have at least once in our lives bought something for our pets to chill out in even though we didn't really like the look of it. Despite this, we let ourselves be persuaded into the purchase against our better judgement, only for the cats to ignore it. A flop all along the line – a classic wrong buy.

⬇ A discarded T-shirt and old wire coat hangers are transformed into an exciting new cat house.

Cats have minds of their own and very fixed ideas about comfort. One loves a worn-out cardboard box more than anything else, while another just can't get enough of a simple doormat.

When you make cat furnishings, pay attention to variations that suit cats, protect the environment by upcycling, and ensure they suit your personal taste. In your hands, old boxes or discarded T-shirts will be given a new lease of life and provide hours of comfort for the cats.

CAT BED

YOU WILL NEED
- [ ] 1 strong cardboard box
- [ ] 1 large discarded T-shirt
- [ ] Cloth tape or biodegradable parcel tape

TO MAKE
1 Fold the flaps of the top of the box to the inside.

2 Pull the T-shirt over the box and pull it into place with the neck opening over the opening of the box and the sleeves at the sides. The neck opening will be the entrance.

3 Turn the sleeves of the T-shirt to the inside and press flat.

4 Fold in the loose T-shirt fabric at the back and fix firmly in place with cloth or parcel tape.

CAT WIGWAM

YOU WILL NEED
- [ ] 2 wire coat hangers
- [ ] Wire cutters
- [ ] Adhesive tape
- [ ] Cardboard
- [ ] Scissors
- [ ] 1 large discarded T-shirt
- [ ] Cloth tape or biodegradable parcel tape

TO MAKE
1 Untwist the curved parts of the coat hangers and use the wire cutters to pinch off the ends below the curly bits.

2 Shape each of the coat hangers into an arc. Make sure that the ends almost form a right angle.

3 Position the arcs so they cross in the middle, then fix the part where they cross firmly with adhesive tape.

4 Measure, mark, then cut the cardboard into a 25cm (10in) square and make a small hole in each corner. Push the loose ends of the wire through the holes and bend them round so they lie as near level as possible with the base.

5 Fix the wire carefully in place with adhesive tape.

6 Pull the T-shirt over the wire frame; the neck opening will become the entrance. Pull everything into shape, fold the sleeves to the inside and use cloth or parcel tape to secure the T-shirt on the underside of the cardboard base.

⬇ The start of a great new cat house is a bold snip with a pair of wire cutters.

⬆ All cats will love this fish: a comfortable retreat made from their absolute favourite material, cardboard.

FRESH FISH ON THE TABLE

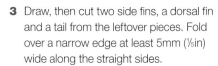

YOU WILL NEED
- ☐ 1 strong cardboard box
- ☐ Adhesive tape
- ☐ Pen or pencil
- ☐ Scissors or Stanley knife

TO MAKE
1 Remove any labels from the box, then bring together and stick the top and bottom flaps with adhesive tape.
2 Draw the open mouth of the fish on either side of one end of the box, then cut it out.
3 Draw, then cut two side fins, a dorsal fin and a tail from the leftover pieces. Fold over a narrow edge at least 5mm (⅕in) wide along the straight sides.
4 To attach the side fins, make slits in the box at the same height on each side, push the edges of the fins through and tape the folded edges in place on the inside. Make similar slits at the top and back for the dorsal fin and tail, and secure in the same way.
5 Lastly, draw on the eyes and fish scales. It's ready to serve!

A-FRAME CABIN

YOU WILL NEED
- [ ] 1 strong cardboard box
- [ ] Adhesive tape
- [ ] Scissors or Stanley knife
- [ ] Saucer
- [ ] Pen or pencil

TO MAKE
1 Carefully remove all fastenings and adhesive tape from the box so you end up with a flat sheet of cardboard.

2 Fold the cardboard into a triangle and fasten the edges together firmly with adhesive tape. Fold the back over and fasten this with tape. Cut any excess cardboard into shape.

3 Using the saucer as a template, draw and then cut a few holes in one side of the box, for peepholes.

Top mouser

Cats have been hunting mice at 10 Downing Street for 500 years. The official name of the position is 'Chief Mouser to the Cabinet Office'. As a civil servant, the cat cannot be dismissed. But why would it be? There's plenty to do in the 500-year-old building. As well as countless mice, even the odd rat has been seen on the steps of the London residence. It has been occupied by prime ministers since 1735 and the office of Chief Mouser has probably existed since the time of Henry VIII (1491–1547).

➡ The current cat occupant of number 10 is Larry, a brown and white tabby.

Go for the unusual

Sometimes it can be quite easy to combine personal taste with the needs of our pets.

Cardboard boxes are not the only things that are perfect for turning into hidey-holes for cats. In principle, anything that is big enough for a cat to get into can be used to make a bed or refuge for them. Do you have an old cupboard that's about to end up in a skip? If it has a drawer of a suitable size then you can fix that to a wall, pop in a few cushions or blankets and you have a unique cat bed. In the same way, with fresh paint and new knobs, an old chest of drawers can be given new life if you reserve one of the drawers for your cats. Maybe they'll like it.

Do you hang on to equipment from previous decades? For instance, is there an old computer gathering dust in the loft?

It will make a fantastic cat house if it's the right size for your pet and the inner workings are removed. You can find

Black cats and the church

In Germany, medieval beliefs still lead to the persecution of black cats, which are more badly treated than others and may end up in animal sanctuaries. During the Inquisition they were associated with the invisible demonic world, probably partly because of their ability to move almost silently and suddenly appear from nowhere. In England, by contrast, black cats have been thought to bring good luck, at least since the break with the Roman Catholic Church, if not before. In 1647, Charles I lamented that his luck had deserted him on the death of his black cat. He was right. The next day, he was arrested and accused of high treason, and he was eventually executed, in 1649.

illustrated step-by-step help for removing the contents on the internet or you can get a professional or a specialist shop to do it for you. Likewise, an eviscerated valve radio will offer an entirely new programme when a cat takes it over. Give free rein to your imagination – you can upcycle a huge number of items to become cat palaces.

Practical advice: when you've had enough of a DIY project, either dispose of it in an environmentally friendly manner or put it away. When you bring it out again, it will be new and interesting again for the cat.

⬇ Take a second glance: you can create unusual cat houses out of all sorts of objects.

LOVE NEVER DIES

One rather inconspicuous item that can very quickly be turned into a piece of cat furniture is the floor cabinet under a washbasin, provided that the hole for the waste pipe is large enough to allow a cat to crawl comfortably inside. The cabinet can be adapted to fit in with your décor with relatively little effort. It is also easy to clean. Practical and attractive to look at – what more can you want?

YOU WILL NEED
- ☐ 1 washbasin cabinet
- ☐ If needed: compass saw (hire service usually available at a DIY store) and sandpaper
- ☐ Optional: paint, paint roller and tray, and doorknobs
- ☐ 1 cushion or blanket, to fit

TO MAKE

1 Turn the cabinet over so that the doors face upwards. The hole for the waste pipe thus becomes the entrance to the cat house.

2 If the hole isn't big enough for your pets, you can widen it using a compass saw. Smooth any rough edges with a piece of sandpaper.

3 Decorate the item with paint and doorknobs to suit your own personal taste and décor.

4 Pop in a cushion or a fleecy blanket and your unusual cat house is finished!

➡ Sometimes you only have to turn something upside down to create unexpected opportunities for new cat houses.

Domesticated tigers

Scientific investigations of cat DNA from various periods during the last 9,000 years have shown that there is very little difference in the genetic make-up of wild cats and domestic cats. The mutation responsible for tabby markings did not appear in domestic cats before the Middle Ages and did not become widespread enough to be associated with domestic cats until the 18th century. Every cat carries the gene for tabby markings, even if the cat appears to be a uniform colour. The plain coat of small kittens often shows the ghost of a pattern that disappears in adulthood. Black cats have tiger stripes that can be seen in certain light conditions.

➡ The markings on Bengal cats show the link between wild and domestic cats.

Make your bed and lie in it

Anyone who sleeps as much and relaxes as stylishly as a cat will very much appreciate somewhere comfortable to repose. To make them feel truly relaxed, however, protection is essential, so positioning is as important as cushioning.

In my experience, our four-legged housemates love giant cushions, the bigger the better. But, as you know, with cats there is always one famous exception that turns every rule upside down and doesn't fit into any category. Let your pet's preferences surprise you and allow them to decide what they like best.

Cats are not only hunters, they are also hunted and therefore are always on the lookout for places that offer protection and safety. As well as cosy comfort, above all a place to sleep must offer refuge and security. For this reason, it's best to make plenty of protection the priority, while at the same time maximising the comfort level.

CAT CUSHION

YOU WILL NEED
- ☐ 1 fleece blanket or discarded large T-shirt
- ☐ 1 cushion
- ☐ Ruler, pen or pencil
- ☐ Scissors or Stanley knife

TO MAKE
1 Lay the fabric out in a double layer, then place the cushion in the centre between the layers. Measure, mark, then cut round the cushion, leaving a margin of about 15cm (6in).

2 Cut fringes about 3cm (2⅕in) wide all round, almost up to the edge of the cushion, with slightly more sloping edges at the corners.

3 Tie pairs of fringes, one upper and one lower, together in a double knot. When all the knots have been tied, trim the fringes to the desired length.

← Lovely knots: it's easy to make something new for your cats even if you don't have superb sewing skills or a sewing machine.

→ It's all a matter of perspective: a cushion may offer an interesting view or be just a place to snooze.

CUDDLY CUSHION: SWEATER GIVEN A NEW LEASE OF LIFE?

Is it time to declutter your wardrobe again? Maybe it's a good opportunity to make an old sweater that's no longer wearable into something cosy to enchant your cats.

YOU WILL NEED

- ☐ 1 large discarded sweater
- ☐ Sewing kit
- ☐ Pins
- ☐ Scissors
- ☐ Toy filler or rags for stuffing

⬅ Reap the fruits of your labours – of course it's even more fun if your super home-made cushion goes down well.

⬆ It's easier than it looks to use needle and thread to make an old favourite sweater into a cosy new favourite spot for the cats.

TO MAKE

1 Turn the sweater the wrong side out and sew up the neck opening. Turn the sweater back to the right side. Pin both sides together in a line across the body below the armholes and sew one line of stitching along this line.

2 Sew the inside edge of the sleeves to the side seams of the body, leaving the armholes open, for stuffing. Now stuff the sleeves with the filler and sew the cuffs shut.

3 Insert a cushion in the tummy or stuff it with more filler or old clothes, then sew up the bottom edge of the sweater.

DREAM TRIP

YOU WILL NEED
- ☐ 1 discarded suitcase
- ☐ 1 cushion or blanket, to fit
- ☐ Optional: fabric, double-sided adhesive tape, scissors, stapler

⬇ Packed your case and going nowhere? Why would you? Home is definitely best!

TO MAKE
1 It could hardly be easier: open the lid of the suitcase and put the cushion or blanket inside.

2 If the lining of the suitcase is not to your taste, you could attach the fabric of your choice to the inside of the suitcase with double-sided adhesive tape. It will be more robust if you also staple it all together in discreet corners.

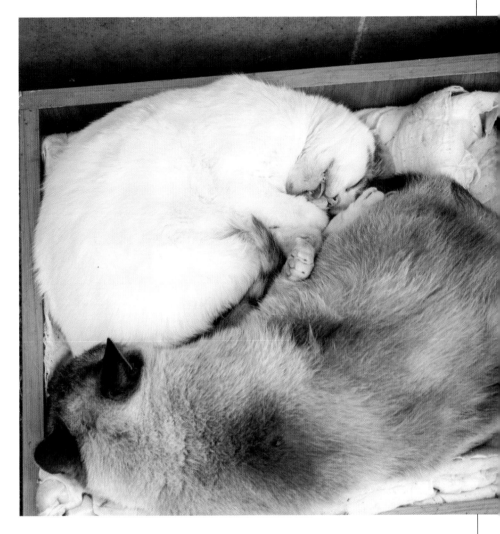

CRATED UP

YOU WILL NEED

- ☐ 1 vegetable or wine crate
- ☐ Sandpaper
- ☐ 1 cushion or blanket, to fit
- ☐ Optional: paint, paint roller

TO MAKE

1 Check the crate and smooth any rough patches or sharp edges with sandpaper.

2 Do you like the crate in its original state? If so, that's great. Just put in a cushion or a cosy blanket and everything's ready for your cat to relax in.

3 You can also adapt the simplest crate with a lick of paint to suit your own personal taste.

LET'S TAKE IT NICE AND EASY

YOU WILL NEED
- [ ] 1 suitable-sized set of shelves or a cupboard
- [ ] Double-sided adhesive tape
- [ ] Sisal rope, 8mm (¹⁄₃in) or thicker
- [ ] If necessary: staple gun
- [ ] Scissors
- [ ] Self-adhesive hook-and-loop fastening (Velcro®)
- [ ] 2 cushions or blankets, to fit

TO MAKE

1 When assembling the shelving, leave off the back, if provided, or remove the back from a cupboard or shelving unit.

2 To make a scratching area, wind double-sided adhesive tape round the top third of one side of the shelving. Wind the rope tightly over the double-sided adhesive tape, fixing the ends in place on the inside of the unit with staples, if necessary.

3 Cut eight equal lengths of self-adhesive hook-and-loop fastening to fit the width of the shelving. Attach two strips to the top of the unit, two strips in the bottom inside, and two strips each on the bottoms of the cushions, so they line up with the strips on the unit.

4 Now just quickly attach the cushions or blankets to the shelving using the hook-and-loop strips. All done!

> **TIP**
>
> *Cats will feel better protected from view if you attach a curtain. That way, they can observe, without being seen (or so they suppose).*

➡ Multi-purpose furniture for our furry friends: practical and pleasant.

Therapeutic purring

Broken bones heal more quickly in cats than in other mammals, due to the fact that purring sets the muscular system into action, which has the effect of stimulating bones to grow. In tests during manned space flight, the use of the cat-purr frequency reduced bone deterioration caused by lack of movement. This may have implications for the treatment of osteoporosis.

Try a little cosiness

Cats are just like the Disney version of Baloo the Bear – always appreciative of the peace and comfort of a cosy home with plenty of places to retreat into, adequate viewpoints from which to spy on the world, and soft padding.

Cats love cosy nooks almost as much as cardboard boxes. They are comfortable places where they can curl up and shut out the outside world. Ideally, they should be spots from which they can keep watch, without (apparently) being seen.

DOUBLE-DECKER CAT

YOU WILL NEED
- [ ] 1 strong cardboard box
- [ ] Adhesive tape
- [ ] Ruler, pen or pencil
- [ ] Scissors or Stanley knife
- [ ] 1 fleece blanket
- [ ] Optional: fabric offcuts, for decorating
- [ ] Double-sided adhesive tape

Variation: Hideaway
Create a much more enclosed space by cutting a single opening, using a cake plate as a template.

YOU WILL NEED
- [ ] Cake plate
- [ ] Pen or pencil
- [ ] Scissors or Stanley knife

TO MAKE
1 Instead of cutting wide openings separated by cardboard pillars, draw round a cake plate in the lower part of the box on one side, then cut it out.

TO MAKE
1 Tape the top and bottom of the box shut with adhesive tape. Tape any protruding bits of cardboard to the box and, if necessary, strengthen torn corners with tape.
2 Measure, mark, then cut out two adjacent sides of the box, leaving an edge measuring 5cm (2in).
3 Measure, mark, then cut 5cm (2in)-long slits in the 'pillars', 10cm (4in) from the top of the box.
4 Cut the fleece blanket to the size of the box plus an allowance of about 10cm (4in). Pull the fleece through the slits, make one cut into each corner of the fleece to create two ties, and knot in place around the pillar.
5 Decorate the box to suit your own taste using fabric offcuts and double-sided adhesive tape.

➡ **Several things that cats like come together here:** a cardboard box, the cosy hanging mat and everything protected from view. Great!

JUST CHILL OUT

YOU WILL NEED

- [ ] 1 strong cardboard box
- [ ] Adhesive tape
- [ ] 1 fleece blanket
- [ ] Ruler, pen or pencil
- [ ] Scissors or Stanley knife
- [ ] Double-sided adhesive tape
- [ ] If necessary: staple gun

TO MAKE

1 Fold the top flaps of the cardboard box completely to the inside and fix in place with cloth or parcel tape. Tidy up and strengthen any torn corners with tape.
2 Place the box on the blanket and measure, mark, then cut around, allowing a margin of 15cm (6in).
3 Wind double-sided adhesive tape around the upper edge of the box, then position the blanket and pull the fabric taut. If necessary, secure in place with staples.
4 Add any further design features you like.

Variation: A state of suspense

Here, a cat can laze on the hanging mat in the box, gazing out at its territory.

YOU WILL NEED

- [ ] Pen or pencil
- [ ] Scissors or Stanley knife
- [ ] Extra fleece blanket
- [ ] Staple gun

TO MAKE

1 Place the box on the blanket and cut around, allowing a margin of 15cm (6in).
2 Secure the fabric in place with staples before continuing from Step 3 above.

← A cosy bed for a cat to laze in is quick to make and an invitation to chill out in comfort.

HULA HOOP

YOU WILL NEED
- [ ] 1 fleece blanket
- [ ] 1 hula hoop or other rigid hoop
- [ ] Scissors
- [ ] Ruler, pen or pencil
- [ ] Sisal rope, 8mm (⅓in) or thicker

TO MAKE
1 Lay the blanket out double and position the hoop in the middle. Measure, mark, then cut all round with an allowance of about 15cm (6in).
2 Cut the allowance in 2.5cm (1in)-wide fringes all the way round, almost to the edge of the hoop.

⬇ A relaxing place to lie in a slightly higher position goes down very well with some cats.

3 Place one layer of fabric under the hoop and the other on top and tie the fringes in pairs, one piece from the top and one from the bottom, with a double knot. Trim the fringes to the desired length.
4 Tie the sisal rope firmly to the hoop in three places (the distance between the knots should be about the same), then join the ends together in a knot.
5 Now just hang it up.

TIP

If you find that the hanging mat swings about too much, take off the ropes, weight the underside with a stone, and replace the ropes. Alternatively, you could place a stone in the fabric before reassembling, which will mean the mat will swing more gently to and fro.

EASY-PEASY HANGING MAT

YOU WILL NEED
- [ ] Ruler, pen or pencil
- [ ] Scissors
- [ ] 1 stretched canvas on a wooden frame, minimum 30 × 40cm (12 x 16in)
- [ ] Fabric, minimum 30 × 40cm (12 x 16in)
- [ ] Double-sided adhesive tape
- [ ] If necessary: staple gun
- [ ] Sisal rope, 8mm (⅓in) or thicker

TO MAKE
1 Measure, mark, then cut a 1.5–2cm (³⁄₅-⁴⁄₅in)-diameter hole in each corner of the canvas, inside the wooden frame.
2 Place the canvas on the fabric and cut the fabric to size, allowing a 5cm (2in) margin all round.
3 Place the fabric on top of the canvas and begin by sticking it to the inside of the frame, where the canvas has been stapled, with the double-sided adhesive tape. If necessary, staple the fabric in place as well.
4 Cut four equal lengths of rope. Pull one through each hole and knot firmly on the underside. Tie the rope together in a thick, firm knot. Hang it up and check it hangs level, adjusting if required.

⬆ Hanging mats for cats save space, offer an elevated viewpoint and are definitely something different for felines to chill out on.

Let's go shopping!

You don't have time for DIY, but you'd still like to extend the options you offer your furry friend? No problem, specialist shops have the answer. Here's one option:

Window lounger – A raised but cosy viewing platform positioned right against the window so cats can watch the world go by. The hanging mat is easily attached to the window with suction cups, which have a fantastic grip if the surface is clean and you test and check the attachment carefully. The wire cords are bite-proof. The product is designed to bear a total weight of 12kg (26½lb). This is sufficient for two cats or one very substantial feline. The covering is easy to remove and is washable at 30°C (86°F).

Welcome home

Scratch around the clock

If the interior furnishings don't meet feline requirements, cats know how to improve things – just not always in ways we especially like.

Cats use visual and scent marking to show other members of their species where they live and what mood they are in. Marks are regularly left in prominent places, in both their outdoor and indoor territory. Scratch marks have acoustic, olfactory and optical effects. The pheromones cats leave with their paws don't carry far; the clearly visible scratch

⬇ Every cat has 18 claws, which they use to help them climb and jump, and for grasping, catching and keeping hold of their prey.

marks work better as messages passed on in this way can still be read days later.

All cats scratch

When leaving important scratch marks, cats are also maintaining their claws. Claws are perfectly designed for climbing, fighting and holding on to prey. Naturally, these unique tools also have to be looked after. The claws are usually retracted when they are not in use – a unique ability in the animal kingdom. Because of this, they don't get blunted, so they don't need to be

sharpened by scratching, as is often assumed. It is much more the case that scratching removes the old claw sheaths when they are worn out, revealing the brand new, sharp claws underneath. The hind paws are licked clean and the old sheaths are picked off with the teeth and chewed up. No scratching is involved.

Scratchmania

What many cat owners fear is that their cat will sink its claws into places they don't want them to and that a new, unwanted design will be transferred to a favourite armchair or a newly papered wall. What exactly is going on when they scratch?

Depending on the cat's preference, scratching may be horizontal, vertical or diagonal. The animal always stands on its hind legs and scratches with its front paws. Incidentally, the mechanism for retracting and extending the claws is trained and strengthened at the same time.

Scratch marks are usually found close to sleeping or resting places or else right at the centre of the territory. Of course, the clever cat doesn't seek out the inconspicuous occasional table but heads straight for a prominent object in its surroundings, such as the sofa, armchair or an upright chair – though only if these are also tempting because they are covered in an attractive material. Sometimes the material of the scratchable object simply isn't to the individual's taste. Cats are motivated by success; they need to achieve a visible result quickly. Out in the wild, they choose trees or objects on which the scratches can be clearly made out. If your pet ignores a wonderful sisal-covered scratching post, perhaps it just doesn't like the material. Owners buy sisal and think, 'Ah, sisal – that's robust. The

Sensitive paws

Mechanoreceptors on the balls of a cat's paws give the animal heightened sensitivity to vibration, so that they really are able to 'hear' with their feet. As a result, even deaf cats are able to sense running mice when they're on the move. This extreme sensitivity is probably one of the reasons why cats react early to natural disasters such as earthquakes.

cat will have to scratch for a long time before we can see anything. Very good.' The cat, meanwhile, may think, 'Ah, sisal – that's robust. I'll have to scratch for a long time before I can see anything. Very stupid.'

It's possible that the feeling of tearing up the material also has a big part to play. Some barks or fibres have an irresistible effect on cats, like our urge to pop bubble wrap when we get our hands on it. Covers with threads that quickly pull, or woodchip wallpaper that shows marks straight away after a short bout of scratching, give the cat an immediate feeling of success and very likely a lovely tactile experience as well. That is probably why many cats favour cardboard scratching toys, and also coconut matting, very soft wood such as pine, or materials made from banana leaves.

So, scratching depends on the favourite material, the direction of scratching and the position of the object. It's amazing that what is apparently such an everyday activity can produce such different, very personal preferences and combinations. But don't worry – you're sure to be able to discover the private passion of your four-legged housemate...

SPIRAL

YOU WILL NEED
- [ ] 1 cardboard box or sheet of cardboard
- [ ] Ruler, pen or pencil
- [ ] Scissors or Stanley knife
- [ ] Solvent-free craft adhesive or glue
- [ ] Leftover wool, parcel string or strips of fabric

TO MAKE
1 Remove all plastic and adhesive tape from the box. Measure, mark, then cut the cardboard into strips roughly 2.5cm (1in) wide.
2 Roll the strips one at a time into a single large, firm spiral, fixing them with craft adhesive or glue as you go along.
3 When the spiral has reached the desired size, glue the end down firmly and tie it all together tightly by winding your chosen wool, string or strips of fabric round it.
4 When the craft adhesive has completely dried, claw sharpening can begin.

Variation: Cardboard in a box

YOU WILL NEED
- [ ] 1 cardboard box, 30 × 15cm (12 x 6in)
- [ ] Ruler, pen or pencil
- [ ] Scissors or Stanley knife
- [ ] Cardboard
- [ ] Solvent-free craft adhesive or glue
- [ ] Leftover wool, parcel string or strips of fabric

➡ Make old into new: home-made scratching toys offer owners a good opportunity to upcycle cardboard and boxes.

TO MAKE

1 Remove all plastic and adhesive tape from the box. Measure, mark, then cut the box to a height of 2.5cm (1in).
2 Cut strips of cardboard to fit the width and height of the box. It is quickest and easiest if you measure and cut one strip and then use this as a template for all the other strips.
3 Spread craft adhesive or glue over the bottom and inner sides of the box, then pack the interior of the box tightly with the strips, standing them vertically on their long edges.
4 Wind your chosen wool, parcel string or strips of fabric round it. Leave to dry completely, then present it to your cat.

There's room in the smallest hut

There are various possible reasons for providing alternative scratching toys in the home. Maybe there just isn't enough space for scratching boards and barrels or perhaps the design of the usual items doesn't suit your personal taste.

YOU WILL NEED
- [ ] Ruler, pen or pencil
- [ ] Scissors or Stanley knife
- [ ] 1 box made of cardboard at least 5mm (⅕in) thick or sheets of normal cardboard doubled over and glued together
- [ ] Drinking glass
- [ ] Solvent-free craft adhesive or glue
- [ ] Gift wrap or wallpaper
- [ ] Double-sided adhesive tape
- [ ] 1 thin coconut or sisal mat
- [ ] If necessary: Tesa® adhesive power strips

TO MAKE
1 Measure, mark, then cut the double-thickness cardboard to a rectangle measuring 15 × 50cm (6 x 20in).
2 Using the drinking glass as a template, draw a circle in the top third of the cardboard and cut it out.
3 Decorate the cardboard according to your own taste by gluing on gift wrap or wallpaper, without covering the hole.
4 Cut the thin coconut or sisal mat to measure 15 × 35cm (6 x 18in), then attach it firmly to the cardboard with the double-sided adhesive tape.
5 Hang the scratching board from a doorknob. For extra security, you may need to fasten the whole thing to the door using Tesa® power strips.

SPACE-SAVER

YOU WILL NEED
- [ ] Double-sided adhesive tape
- [ ] Sisal rope, 8mm (⅓in) or thicker
- [ ] Scissors

TO MAKE
1 You will definitely save space if you convert a table or chair leg into a scratching post. (Please remember that adhesive tape may damage furniture.) You can also give a suitable indoor plant a new function if it is tall and stable enough for a cat sharpen its claws on.
2 Encase some of the table or chair leg or plant in double-sided adhesive tape, then wind the sisal rope very firmly over it and press to secure.

➡ Providing numerous opportunities for scratching in various places around the home can prevent undesired scratching.

Catisfaction

Cats are totally committed to washing – it's part and parcel of their world and an absolute must in terms of maintaining their health and well-being. Stroking, meanwhile, is an expression of affection and is beneficial for humans and cats alike.

The short, not very thorough, wash that we think of when we use the expression 'cat lick' does not correspond to the method and function of what cats actually do. Every day, cats spend 10–30 per cent of their time on personal hygiene. They start practising early in life; the washing instinct can be seen in young kittens immediately after birth, and from the second week they begin to wash themselves independently.

Cat hygiene not only rids the fur of dirt and smells and keeps it sleek, but it also stimulates the sebaceous glands to secrete sebum into the hair follicles and skin, impregnating the fur and protecting the skin from water. A dishevelled coat is poor protection against the cold and makes the cat more susceptible to infection. In summer, grooming the fur functions as air-conditioning. Like dogs, cats don't have sweat glands spread all over their bodies. As panting achieves little in the way of cooling, cats spread as much saliva as possible over their bodies; it then evaporates and thus protects them

against overheating. That's why they wash more frequently in summer than in winter.

Washing is a pleasure

Surprisingly, personal hygiene actually helps cats to remain even-tempered, as it stimulates the release of endorphins. These so-called 'happy hormones' have a relaxing effect and relieve anxiety. If a cat is prevented from grooming its fur, perhaps because it has to wear a recovery collar or it is unfortunately so fat that it can no longer wash its whole body itself, it may cause great stress that increases with time. Just imagine the torment of not being able to scratch an itch. In conflict situations, a cat will quickly lick its mouth or wash itself – we humans touch our faces or heads. Mutual grooming supports animals in reducing social tension and establishing friendships.

Everything in the right order

The washing sequence is always the same: from front to back. For the most part, cats use their rough tongue, licking intensively to clean the fur. For the head and face, they moisten a paw with saliva and use it as a facecloth because their tongue can't reach these areas.

Cats wash after meals and before and after periods of rest or sleep. Most cats also start intensive grooming immediately after being stroked. For one thing, the fur needs to be put straight. In addition, their own smell has been masked by our scent. Who knows whether cats clean themselves at this point in order to re-establish their own smell as quickly as possible or whether they like the taste of us? Maybe both theories are correct.

◄ Typical cat: thorough washing and extensive sleeping and resting every day are extremely important to a cat's well-being.

Sun worshipper

In newborn kittens, as well as the sense of hearing, awareness of warmth develops particularly early. The heat receptors next to the nose inform the tiny creatures, which are blind and deaf to begin with, where to find the mother and siblings that they must cuddle up to in order to obtain the warmth they need to stay alive. The love of warmth remains with them throughout their lives. Their fur can reach temperatures of more than 50°C (122°F) without any harm coming to them. Nevertheless, there should always be a shady place where they can cool off.

Tiny hooks

All cats' tongues are furnished with a number of tiny barbs; each individual hook on these is movable and is erected during washing. This means that even stubborn dirt can be removed and knotty tufts of hair untangled. After grooming, the barbs are laid flat and wiped towards the throat in order to clean the tongue. That must be the reason why tufts of hair are spat out.

Cuddly kittens

Most cats like to snuggle up to their owners – provided that this happens when they feel like it. Some cats are insatiable snugglers that can't be stroked enough, while others are satisfied with a fleeting touch.

Bonds are formed by cuddling; cosying up together mingles scents and creates a common group smell that strengthens the

⬇ That's why we love them: for many cat-owners, cuddling up to one another is the best part of living with cats.

sense of solidarity and conveys a feeling of security. If your cat snuggles up to you, it is treating you as one of its own kind and showing you its affection. If it shows you a cheek or its tummy, it is demonstrating its trust, regardless of whether it allows these parts to be stroked briefly, for a long time, or not at all. The neck and the sensitive tummy area are among the parts that cats protect and rarely expose in the wild.

Stroking quite literally gets under the cat's skin. Each individual hair is linked to mechanoreceptors that transmit information to the brain about the surrounding world. In many cats, cuddling lowers the pulse and causes the muscles to relax. It has a similar positive effect on humans: blood pressure and pulse rate go down and the happy hormone serotonin is released. Cuddling is a classic win-win situation all along the line.

Should I stay or should I go?

Cats are constantly maligned as being treacherous and disloyal, probably mainly because some of them snuggle up lovingly one minute and then, for no apparent reason, go completely mad and mutate into spitfires. This ambivalent behaviour is likely the result of overexcitement, due to the fact that the neural pathways conveying the pleasant sensation created by stroking also transmit the sensation of pain. Imagine the following: you have an itch, scratching relieves it and makes you feel better. But if you keep scratching the same place, it is not only unpleasant but also soon starts to feel painful.

Cats let you know when it's getting too much for them, although to human eyes they often communicate so subtly that the fleeting signals from your lap are overlooked. Some cats simply turn away, others stand up and walk off. Those are really clear signals. Many just stiffen their body; some twitch only the tip of their tail, while with others the entire tail lashes wildly to and fro. Some place a paw on your hand, while many raise a paw as a warning. Sometimes, they will bite your hand, usually very gently, which is why this signal is affectionately known as a 'love bite'.

Pay heed to these signals and stop caressing too early rather than too late, even if you're still enjoying it. If the cat's warning phase is continually ignored, it may use increasingly aggressive methods to try to stop the stroking. As a result, it will learn that hissing, snarling, scratching and a bite that is no longer gentle are the only possible ways to escape from unwelcome cuddling. In addition, the warning phase may be so much curtailed that it seems as if the cat is suddenly striking out for no reason.

When you were little, did you like it when your relatives went on squeezing, kissing and cuddling you for too long? There you have it.

Cat therapy

Cats help to combat human depression and stress and they are brilliant at inducing relaxation. It has been scientifically proved that regular contact with cats has the same therapeutic effect as psychological relaxation techniques.

GROOMING CENTRE

Grooming and brushing stimulate the circulation, which may reduce hair loss. Cats usually change their coat in spring and autumn, although indoor cats generally shed fewer hairs – even if it doesn't seem like that when you're living with them.

YOU WILL NEED
- ☐ 1 radiator brush, 75cm (30in) long
- ☐ 1 vegetable brush or nailbrush with a smooth back
- ☐ Extra-strong adhesive
- ☐ Wooden board, 50 × 50cm (20 x 20in)

TO MAKE
1 Bend the radiator brush into an arc and glue it and the other brush on to the wooden board.
2 Set it up and 'yippee' – all finished!

Variation: Space-saving hair-care centre

YOU WILL NEED
- ☐ 1 vegetable brush or nailbrush with a smooth back
- ☐ Extra-strong adhesive

TO MAKE
1 Glue the brush to the corner of a wall or the leg of a table or chair, then leave it to dry completely. Your cat is sure to enjoy rubbing against it.

← Sometimes it can be as easy as this to provide your cat with another grooming opportunity.

Hairy

The average density of cats' hair is an impressive 25,000 per sq cm (0.16 sq in). By way of comparison, dogs have 1,000–9,000 hairs and humans 175–350 hairs per sq cm (0.16 sq in).

Splish-splash

The average fluid requirement of a cat is around 60–80ml (2–2¾fl oz) per 1kg (2.2lb) of body weight – depending on nutrition, individual activity and ambient temperature.

Cats obtain the majority of their fluid requirement from consuming moist food. Nevertheless, they need to drink as well in order to prevent diseases of the urinary tract or kidneys. This is particularly important if they mostly eat dry food. To stimulate drinking, it is best to have water available in several places and to check that food and water are consumed in different places.

DRINK, KITTY, DRINK

YOU WILL NEED
- ☐ Ruler, pen
- ☐ Bradawl, pointed scissors or small, sharp kitchen knife
- ☐ 1 small PET plastic bottle with lid
- ☐ 1 non-tip bowl

TO MAKE
1 Meaure, mark, then carefully bore a very small hole in the bottle about 2.5–5cm (1–2in) above the bottom. The level of the opening depends on how high you want the water level in the bowl to be once you've filled it.

2 Keep your finger over the hole while you fill the bottle with water.

3 Screw the cap on tightly, stand the bottle in the bowl, then quickly fill the bowl with water so that it comes to a level just above the hole.

4 Raise a cheer for low pressure! This prevents the bowl from filling with an uncontrolled amount of water from the bottle. As the water level in the bowl sinks as the cat drinks, more water flows out into the bowl from the bottle until the hole is once again covered and the flow stops.

➡ A very simple project for upcycling a plastic bottle and offering your cat another place to drink at home.

⬇ This simple drinking fountain is particularly suitable for a multi-cat household and also on hot days.

BUBBLING WATER

YOU WILL NEED

- [ ] 1 hose, 10mm (⅖in) diameter
- [ ] 1 12-volt drinking fountain pump
- [ ] 1 clay flowerpot
- [ ] Scissors
- [ ] 1 non-tip clay saucer or bowl (size to suit the pot)

TO MAKE

1 Attach the hose to the drinking fountain pump outlet, push it through the hole in the bottom of the flowerpot and cut it off above the rim.

2 Place the pot and the pump upside down in the saucer or bowl, leaving the cable hanging safely over the edge.

3 Fill the saucer or bowl with water, switch on the current and watch the water spurt gently out of the top of the tube.

Spoon-wise

Scientific research has shown that cats create a column of water that they briefly bite with their tongue, taking up water with their tongue formed into a spoon shape. Drops of water remain clinging to the millions of filiform papillae that are found on the tongue and can thus be transported further into the throat.

➡ Many cats love drinking, watching and pawing at bubbling water. It's easy to find out if the same is true of your cats.

⬇ You really don't have to be a hugely talented DIY buff to conjure up this great drinking fountain for your cats!

Welcome to the meadows

Outdoor cats naturally nibble various grasses to aid digestion. Since green matter is not available in flats, you need to give indoor cats a helping hand.

Cats need more than just vitamins and minerals for their well-being; they also need roughage, which is important for digestion.

Grass offers this, along with nutrients, so growing your own green matter provides nourishment, roughage and activity all in one.

GROWING CAT GRASS WITHOUT SOIL

YOU WILL NEED
- [ ] Container of your choice
- [ ] Material for filling: pebbles, shells or marbles
- [ ] 1 unbleached coffee filter
- [ ] Cat grass seed

TO MAKE
1 Fill the container about three-quarters full with pebbles, shells or marbles, then place the coffee filter on top, so that everything is well covered. Leave a small margin free at the top.

2 Spread a thin layer of seed evenly over the filter and fill the container up with water as far as the filter.

3 Keep topping the water up to the level of the filter during the first few days, until the roots sprout. This will help the seeds to sprout more quickly. When the green grass appears, avoid drowning it.

4 After 7–10 days, the grass is ready.

← ↓ Little effort, great effect: fresh green matter to smell and nibble is particularly important for cats that are never able to go outdoors.

Variation: The grass is usually greener

YOU WILL NEED
- [ ] Organic cotton wool pads
- [ ] 1 shallow bowl
- [ ] Cat grass seed

TO MAKE
1 Arrange a layer of cotton wool pads in a shallow bowl and spread the seeds evenly over them. Water the pads to moisten, then keep them moist until the seeds sprout. When the green grass appears, don't overwater it.

TIP

It is best to buy very fine, small-grained seed (1mm) that roots very firmly, so the cat doesn't uproot it immediately. If you want to use a glass jar or ceramic bowl as a container, take particular care to ensure it will be stable and secure when a cat leans on it while grazing on the grass. If it falls and smashes on the floor, your cat could be seriously injured.

IN THE GREEN MEADOW

YOU WILL NEED

- [ ] 1 small set of shelves or a cupboard (no smaller than 35 × 35 × 70cm/ 14 x 14 x 28in), without doors
- [ ] Double-sided adhesive tape
- [ ] Sisal rope, 8mm (⅓in) or thicker
- [ ] If necessary: staple gun
- [ ] Electric drill (hire service usually available at a DIY store)
- [ ] Router (hire service usually available at a DIY store)
- [ ] Strong waterproof foil
- [ ] Herb substrate
- [ ] Cat grass seed
- [ ] Scissors
- [ ] Self-adhesive hook-and-loop fastening (Velcro®)
- [ ] Cushion or blanket, to fit
- [ ] Optional: fabric for a small curtain

TO MAKE

1 When assembling the shelves, leave off the back, if provided, or remove the back from an item of furniture you already have.

2 Carefully wind double-sided adhesive tape round the top third of one side of the shelving.

3 Press the sisal rope very firmly and close together on the double-sided adhesive tape. If necessary, strengthen and secure the ends by stapling them in place on the inside of the shelf.

4 Carefully drill a small hole in the top plank of the shelving. Insert the router in the hole and carefully hollow out an area for the grass, which should cover no more than half the total length of the top. Take care not to drill any more holes in the wood.

5 Fix the foil in the hollow with double-sided adhesive tape. If necessary, staple carefully around the edge.

6 Fill the hollow with herb substrate, then sow and water the cat grass according to the instructions.

7 Cut eight lengths of self-adhesive hook-and-loop fastening to fit the width of the shelving. Stick pairs of the fastening strips to the top and bottom parts of the shelves and attach two strips to each cushion or blanket.

8 Attach the cushion or blanket firmly to the shelves with the hook-and-loop fastening so they will not slip.

9 If liked, you can cover the lower 'den' with a fabric curtain.

➡ **Multi-functional: here, cats can chill out, observe, nibble grass or scratch as the fancy takes them.**

A good place to be!

Cats are the only animals to have chosen to become both domestic pets and working animals. During the Neolithic period, they kept close to agricultural communities, where there was an abundance of mice and rats – attracted by cereals and other crops. All the other domesticated animals around us have been bred selectively to fulfil specific tasks.

Forever
fun

Solo entertainer

When we know what and how cats hunt in the wild and put this knowledge into practice in our homes, albeit in a modified form, our pets are less likely to get bored, even when we're out for long periods of time.

'Whoever is not curious will learn nothing.' This aphorism may have occurred to Goethe while watching his cat. Cats have an unerring memory for locality. On their daily patrols of their territory, not even the slightest change escapes them. They use their sight, hearing and particularly their sense of smell for orientation. All the impressions from these fit together in a cognitive plan that helps them to find their bearings in the world around them. Their knowledge of the position of everything is so precise that they could manage with their eyes shut.

The location of an object is linked to a designation. If the object moves to a different place, it loses its previous meaning. This may be problematic, for example, if the litter tray is moved and they no longer make use of it in its new position. However, of course this doesn't mean that you're not allowed to make any change in the home environment. It is simply important to maintain stable structures while also allowing a certain amount of change, so the surroundings continue to be meet cats' cognitive and territorial needs. This makes sense – after all, we don't completely change every room in our home every day as we too find it hard to adapt to new arrangements. If our new bathroom has an entirely different layout, for example, we will definitely have one or two initial problems with finding our way around – particularly when we're not wide awake, such as at night.

If you're always on the move, there are one or two things you can do to ensure that your cats are happily occupied when they're alone, so they can stop thinking about your absence. Designing their home terrain with an eye to environmental enrichment will make it more interesting and exciting; a lovely scratching tree, interesting views from the window, a variety of chances to climb, places to hide, opportunities to hunt and the right feline friend will suit cats perfectly.

The cat that walks by itself

Cats are still often thought of as loners. They hunt alone, which is appropriate, given the small size of their prey, but otherwise they like to have company around them. Outdoor cats specifically seek out bosom pals to hang around with on their expeditions. Some feline friends even collect each other from their homes before going off on a tour.

Most cats benefit from having a suitable feline friend; it's great for snuggling up together, playing, quarrelling, chilling out and passing the time. Of course it all depends on individual needs and personal taste. They don't always lie down together as in the photos on cat calendars, but often snooze in completely different areas of the home environment.

➡ Environmental enrichment enables cats to follow their natural behaviour patterns within their own four walls.

← Know-how: cats are most likely to play with toys that closely resemble their natural prey, and that are easy to pick up and bat around.

Members of the same species are the best and simplest insurance against boredom and its possible consequences. Feline company is beneficial for almost all cats that have to stay at home alone for more than four or five hours every day.

Home games

Spotting prey, lying in wait and pursuit are all part of an outdoor cat's strolls around its territory. Life without hunting would be dead boring for these instinctive hunters. While you are out of the house, give them an opportunity for playful stalking within their own four walls.

Form follows function: the more a toy resembles cats' natural prey, the more likely it is to trigger play. To make it even more like their prey, it should be easy to manipulate with the paws and not make too loud a noise.

Mice are obviously among the favourite prey animals, but insects, slow worms, lizards and whatever is to be found in the cat's living space are also on the menu. A mouse is about the size of a thumb, so use this as a guide when choosing toys. Toys that are too large not only fall outside the spectrum of prey but can even cause anxiety. Not all cats are lion-hearted enough to hunt rats.

Apart from providing the right toys, there are a few other things that can be done in order to make life without humans more interesting. If the toy prey just lies around on the floor, it's rather dull – the excitement of pursuit is lacking. If the cat discovers the prey on its usual patrol of the indoor territory, it will be

Lone cats

Very few cats don't get on with other members of their own species. When they don't, it's usually because they were separated far too early from their mother and siblings. This means that they didn't have a proper chance to learn how felines communicate within a group and, as a result, they appear aggressive to other members of the species because they are unable to respond appropriately to their placatory signals. The longer cats that are allowed to remain with their mother and siblings, the better their social abilities in later life. The earliest time for separation is around 12 weeks. Cats should always live closely together with other cats and the simplest way to achieve this is with littermates.

more exciting. So, hide new or well-known items, cat treats or dry food on your pet's regular routes around its territory and give it something to hunt out.

Awaken the hunting instinct in your cat. Maybe bring something back from your next walk and let the cat discover it as it roams around the home: acorns, walnuts, hazelnuts, beech mast (nuts) and small feathers match the size of prey perfectly. If you rinse feathers in hot water, you won't have any worries about hygiene. Little gifts such as leaves, hay, small twigs, shells, stones or sand tell stories of the world outside. Cats can smell out this potpourri of scents with their excellent noses.

Tailor-made toys

Playthings that you have made yourself or collected are great, because you know exactly where they have come from and what's inside them. However, sometimes you don't have time for that. Luckily, there are also wonderful things available to buy that make perfect toys:

■ Small felt balls, about 1.5cm (³/₅in) in diameter. These balls are quick and easy to send flying around and are

not dangerous if they are picked up in the mouth.
■ Unshelled peanuts are the right size, light and excellent for flicking around.
■ Uncooked pasta such as macaroni and spirals are the perfect size, and if a cat should decide to nibble them, no harm will be done.
■ Toy mice without plastic insides, eyes or noses are a standard purchase from the pet shop.
■ Balls bounce excitingly, but if they smell too artificial it's better to leave them in the shop. Softening agents may have been used in their manufacture.

If you get a sudden urge to make something yourself, cats will be delighted by these:

■ Small, very firm paper balls. Please don't use newspaper, as inks may run when moistened and will possibly be unhealthy for your cat.
■ Wine corks cut in half bounce rather more randomly, which makes them more interesting.
■ Unpacked tampons with shortened strings are very tempting.
■ Balls from old deodorant rollers.

Cat watch?

In a one-week investigation, the BBC studied 50 cats using special cat cameras. The study showed that the animals spent only 20 per cent of their time outside and a few never went out at all. A total of 20 prey animals were killed, an average of half a victim per cat – far fewer than expected. A similar experiment by the German broadcasting company SWR produced comparable results. More cats than expected gorged on food in neighbours' houses – a new adaptation of stalking.

All alone

An environment that meets the needs of cats will not only be appropriate to the species but will also enable them to fill small periods of time. Safety (see also page 14 and below) is particularly important while you are out, as you won't be present to intervene quickly.

⬇ Most cats enjoy playing with a wide variety of toys, when they are in the right mood.

■ Watch your cat playing with a new toy before leaving them alone with it. Problems may arise that you would never have thought of.

■ Quality is the be-all and end-all. Look at the materials – remove sharp edges, very small plastic parts and items that may easily become detached. Ensure that the cat can't nibble any plastic and wood won't splinter.

■ Keep toys that have become boring in an inaccessible place – for example, in a box with a lid. When you offer them to your cat again after a while they will have become interesting once more.

■ Less is more: of course your furry companion needs something to pat about and hunt when it feels like playing and you aren't there, but too many incentives may have the opposite effect.

■ Seeking and thinking games: cats have an unbridled passion for stalking. Seeking and thinking games make a good substitute when you are out.

Toys for lonely hours

Many toys can be made in moments from things you will usually have in the house in any case. Just experiment to find out what appeals most to your cat.

FEATHER LIGHT

YOU WILL NEED
- [ ] Ruler, pen or pencil
- [ ] Scissors or Stanley knife
- [ ] Cardboard
- [ ] Feathers you have collected
- [ ] Leftover wool, parcel string or strips of fabric

TO MAKE
1 Measure, mark, then cut the cardboard into 2.5 × 7.5cm (1 x 3in) pieces.
2 Place a feather on the card and wrap it tightly with wool, string or fabric strips.

TIP

If the feathers are too big, simply use scissors to trim them to fit. Be careful with bought feathers: often, you can't tell where they have come from and colourful feathers that have been dyed may be unsuitable for decoration or even poisonous.

⬇ Less is sometimes more: feathers you have collected yourself, a piece of cardboard and some string produce a simple but effective toy.

Variation: Shuttlecock

YOU WILL NEED
- ☐ 3–5 small or medium-sized feathers
- ☐ Leftover wool, parcel string or strips of T-shirt fabric
- ☐ If necessary: scissors and ruler

TO MAKE
1. Tie the feathers very tightly together around the shafts with wool, string or fabric strips.
2. Turn the feathers so that they curve outwards.
2. Trim off the quills just below where they are tied.
4. If necessary, shorten the feathers to a length of 5–6cm (2–2⅜in).

⬆ Really simple and made in no time: a small woollen pompom.

SMALL POMPOM

YOU WILL NEED
- ☐ 1 table fork
- ☐ Leftover wool
- ☐ Scissors

TO MAKE
1. Wind the wool around the whole width of the fork, then tie a strand around the middle of the wool and knot tightly.
2. Pull the wool off the fork, then carefully cut through the loops on either side of the central knot. Trim the pompom to the desired size and that's it.

⬆ These amusing balls are an uncomplicated but effective way of keeping pets occupied.

KEEP THE BALL ROLLING

YOU WILL NEED
- ☐ Ruler, pen or pencil
- ☐ Scissors or Stanley knife
- ☐ 1 empty toilet roll tube
- ☐ To fill: large cat treats or small feathers

TO MAKE
1 Measure, mark, then cut the tube into four rings, about the width of a finger or 1.5–2cm (^{3}/$_5$–^{4}/$_5$in) wide.
2 Place the rings inside one another to form a ball shape.
3 Fill the ball with cat treats or a small feather. That's it – all done!

➡ An empty cardboard box is often enough to keep your cat entertained or interested.

DOUBLE HELIX

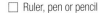

YOU WILL NEED
- [ ] Ruler, pen or pencil
- [ ] Scissors or Stanley knife
- [ ] 1 empty toilet roll tube

TO MAKE
1 Measure, mark, then cut the tube into 1cm (²⁄₅in) strips.
2 Roll each strip into a small spiral, then pull it out a little way at both ends. Press the ends together to produce a slight spiral shape.
3 Throw the strips to your cat.

BOW

YOU WILL NEED
- [ ] Ruler, pen or pencil
- [ ] Scissors or Stanley knife
- [ ] 1 empty toilet roll tube
- [ ] Leftover wool, parcel string or strips of T-shirt fabric

TO MAKE
1 Measure, mark, then cut 0.5–1cm (¹⁄₅–²⁄₅in)-wide rings from the tube.
2 Press each ring in the middle and tie the string around it to make a bow shape, leaving trailing ends for extra fun.

⬇ A simple but entertaining toy: firm yet flexible, small but can't be swallowed, easy to toss around.

ALONG CAME A SPIDER

YOU WILL NEED
- [ ] 1 plastic ring cut from the widest part of a plastic drink bottle
- [ ] If necessary: adhesive tape
- [ ] 1 discarded T-shirt
- [ ] Ruler, pen or pencil
- [ ] Scissors

TO MAKE

1 If necessary, stick the ring together with adhesive tape.

2 Measure, mark, then cut the fabric into 20 or so 1 x 7.5cm (²/₅in x 3in) strips.

3 Tie all of the fabric strips round the ring with a firm double knot. You will need about 20 strips per ring to fill it all the way round.

⬇ Upcycling is trendy – lots of cats will think so too, when they are given lovely new toys to play with.

Variation: Ring-a-ding

YOU WILL NEED
- [ ] 1 plastic ring cut from the widest part of a plastic drink bottle
- [ ] If necessary: adhesive tape
- [ ] 1 discarded T-shirt
- [ ] Ruler, pen or pencil
- [ ] Scissors

TO MAKE

1 Stick the ring together with adhesive tape if necessary.

2 Measure, mark, then cut the fabric into 15–20cm (6–8in)-long strips, 1cm (²/₅in) wide. Make them as long as possible.

3 Knot one end of each strip very tightly to the ring and wind it firmly round all the plastic. Repeat until no more plastic can be seen.

4 Lastly, tie everything firmly and trim off the excess fabric.

⬆ Many cats find the exciting noise made by individual pieces of cardboard rubbing against one another particularly interesting and enjoyable.

CORKSCREW

YOU WILL NEED

- ☐ Ruler, pen or pencil
- ☐ Scissors or Stanley knife
- ☐ Cardboard or 1 empty toilet roll tube
- ☐ Leftover wool, parcel string or strips of T-shirt fabric

TO MAKE

1 Measure, mark, then cut the cardboard into 3 × 5cm (1⅕ x 2in) pieces. each one tightly to form a small tube.

2 Roll up each cardboard tube tightly to form a small tube.

3 Tie the wool, parcel string or strips of fabric tightly round the middle and knot several times. It's as easy as that!

TWISTER

YOU WILL NEED

- [ ] Pen or pencil
- [ ] 1p coin
- [ ] Cardboard
- [ ] Scissors or Stanley knife
- [ ] Wool yarn or parcel string, length approx. 20cm (4in)

TO MAKE

1 Draw round the coin several times on the cardboard, then cut out the circles.

2 Using the scissors or knife, carefully make a hole in the middle of each circle.

3 Thread four card circles on to the yarn or parcel string. Tie three or four knots in the yarn or string on either side of the circles and cut off the ends if they are too long.

⬇ A mouse made from pieces of cardboard that rustle excitingly soon arouses the hunting instinct and stimulates play.

Variation: Mouse

YOU WILL NEED

- [ ] Pen or pencil
- [ ] 1p and 5p coins, plus a coin or washer 16mm (³/₅in) diameter
- [ ] Cardboard
- [ ] Scissors or Stanley knife
- [ ] Wool yarn or parcel string, length approx. 20cm (4in)

TO MAKE

1 Draw round the coins and/or washer on the cardboard. For one mouse toy you will need four circles of each different size. Using the scissors or knife, make a hole in the middle of each circle.

2 Thread the circles on to the string in the following order: 2 × 16mm (³/₅in), 2 × 5p, 4 × 1p, 2 × 16mm (³/₅in).

3 Knot the string on either side of the circles. Cut off after the knot at one end and leave 5cm (2in) at the other end for the tail. Tie a couple of knots in the end.

KNOTTY PROBLEM

YOU WILL NEED
- [ ] Ruler, pen or pencil
- [ ] Scissors
- [ ] 1 discarded T-shirt

TO MAKE

1 Measure, mark, then cut out pieces of fabric measuring 5 × 10cm (2 x 4in).

2 Fold each piece lengthwise and tie a knot in the middle. Trim away on either side of the knot to leave an overall length of about 5cm (2in).

Variation: Tentacles

YOU WILL NEED
- [ ] Ruler, pen or pencil
- [ ] Scissors
- [ ] 1 discarded T-shirt

TO MAKE

1 Measure, mark, then cut out six–eight thin strips of T-shirt fabric measuring 10cm (4in) long.

2 Place all apart from one of the strips one on top of the other in a star shape.

3 Use the last strip to tie all the other strips together very tightly.

4 Tie a knot in each strip close to the end.

← Using simple methods, a discarded T-shirt can very quickly and easily be made into an interesting upcycled toy.

Purring speed

Cats purr about 1,500 times per minute. During their lifetime, cats purr for an average of 10,950 hours.

Just like heaven

Resistance is futile

However good it is to be able to chill out in uninterrupted peace, at the end of the day, nothing beats playing with one's favourite humans.

It used to be assumed that cats formed an attachment only to their territory. However, science has long since proved that they build up very close ties to their human companions. Cats are the only pets that have a close relationship with those who feed them but nevertheless retain their overall independence.

Because we take over the functions of the mother cat in the home – keeping the nest clean, grooming and feeding – the cats who live with us behave like small kittens. In the feline family unit, they miaow when they feel cold or abandoned – an alarm signal for the mother cat, who reacts promptly. We also react very swiftly to miaowing, as the plaintive sound has a similar frequency to the crying of a baby. Cats quickly learn what particular noises their owners react to, how they respond and the best way to manipulate them. If a particular miaow has proved successful, it will, of course, continue to be used in future. Both miaowing and purring are used for specific purposes, as a high-pitched miaow is embedded in the deep, purring noise. The vocalisation of domestic cats is different from that of feral cats. This may be a sign that the relationship with humans has an influence on 'cat language'.

You've got a friend

Cats reacting affectionately to your caressing hand behave exactly as they do to other members of their own species: they erect their tail as a sign of friendship, and rub against, sit beside and wash their people, just as they do with one another.

We point to things when we're chatting – a typically human gesture. Naturally, we communicate in the same way with cats. We can't change our spots any more than cats can. Scientific studies have shown that cats can follow human gestures in order to find food. And that's not all: in dangerous situations, they turn to the person they trust. In the human social referencing process, children check with their parents and thus learn that in unfamiliar situations they need not be afraid if the people they trust do not appear anxious. Cats, too, keep a close eye on people and react to their emotions – social referencing also exists among felines.

Dogs live in packs, humans in family groups – there are certain similarities in this. By contrast, cats are social loners that alter their behaviour to be socially compatible with humans, which reveals a great capacity for adaptation. This is not only an astonishing accomplishment and a sign of

Purrfect

A mother cat uses purring to tell her newborn offspring where she is, as they are blind and deaf to begin with. Kittens purr from the first week of their life, a signal to the mother that all's well.

➡ Cats show their love in quite different ways: by nuzzling, milk treading or simply by being near us.

great intelligence, but something that is also grasped extremely quickly by our favourite pets. According to the cat specialist Dennis C. Turner, the behaviour of humans and cats has all the marks of a true social partnership: the more the owner fulfils the wishes of the

🔻 Playing with humans is just perfect! It creates trust, ensures appropriate relaxation and is enormous fun.

cat (through play, stroking, talking and feeding), the more willing the cat is to fulfil the owner's wishes. Scientific studies have shown that over the years, people and cats develop a relationship that is very similar to the behaviour patterns, rituals and routines of an old married couple.

Sometimes, though, the relationship with the human becomes a little too close, which may in some circumstances lead to

separation anxiety. One or two other factors may make anxiety problems in later life more likely, for instance being separated too early from the mother cat. Of course, not every animal with an increased risk actually develops psychological problems.

All a matter of time

Having a close relationship with a human means that a cat likes to spend time with its

owner. This is great, but it does mean that too much time spent alone does not go down well. Four–five hours is the daily maximum for an indoor cat that has no feline companions. If there are two animals, things look a little different – but even then the daily maximum without humans should not really be more than 10–12 hours. This just shows the advantage of two cats living together: less boredom for the animals and double the pleasure for the owner.

Although the absence of humans is normally used for recuperative napping, of course cats do not sleep the whole time they are unaccompanied. Movement and activity are called for during the waking periods. An environment that contains attractive games and toys to keep them occupied, ample retreats and interesting views provide splendid ways of occupying the time while people are out. That's fine, and means there's no pressing need for cats to turn the place upside down out of boredom. However, in the long term, neither the most wonderful surroundings nor the best feline companion can replace time spent with the human who feeds them.

Brigadier Broccoli

In 2005, this tabby cat took up residence in the Swiss army base in Lyss and a few years ago she was officially registered as being in service with the Swiss army. This makes Broccoli one of three registered cats in the Swiss Confederation. Her two furry colleagues have been officially employed to hunt mice, while the tabby has no formal occupation and is simply there to create a good atmosphere.

Simply the best

Playing chase and seek is a wonderful substitute for hunting indoors. A toy fishing rod is one of the best ways to simulate the thrill of the chase in a way that will keep your cat mentally and physically fit and strengthen the bond between you.

Hunting is one of the most important activities for outdoor cats and can easily occupy up to 10 hours of the day. Some 10–20 mice will be killed during this period. Without the daily hunt, a cat that lives entirely indoors will have a great deal of pent-up energy. For the born hunter, play is the best substitute for stalking in the wild – plus it is enjoyable and helps cats to relax.

During the day, a good spread of games ensures the best use of available time and space. Several shorter play sessions are more beneficial than one very long evening session of play with your pets. The latter is not natural for cats, as they are sprinters rather than marathon runners and need time for regeneration after activity. It makes sense, then, to play before you leave home; a tired cat will be less inclined to get up to mischief and will be twice as happy to rest while you are out.

Little teeth

Bite inhibition prevents siblings from injuring one another during play fighting. This mental block is normally overcome during hunting. If not, cats will only play around with their prey. However, the inhibition threshold is usually abolished on the principle of 'now or never' and the mouse is killed if another cat wants to snatch it away. Competition is good for business.

From the cat's point of view, when you play with it you are taking on the role of the mother cat playfully teaching kittens how to hunt – an activity that will keep them physically and mentally fit. Because of the close relationship cats have with humans, they prefer it if their favourite biped is holding the fishing rod and ineracting with them, rather than playing alone with some automatically spinning toy.

What makes a good fishing rod?

The more key stimuli a fishing rod provides, the more attractive it becomes. Depending on what the mother has brought to the nest, the kittens may develop a preference for a particular kind of prey: mice, insects, birds, snakes and so on. So, the bait on a fishing rod should match the preferred type of prey as far as possible.

In addition, the kind of game the rod is used for is important. When you're playing with your cat, move the rod to make the prey act as realistically as possible; this will appeal to various senses and trigger the hunting instinct. A wider circle of activity often helps. It's an advantage for us, too, as we don't have to move so much with this kind of fishing and it's not so hard on our backs. Cats react to movements that quickly disappear from their field of vision. Understandably, a mouse scampers off and hides when it encounters a cat. Imitate this behaviour by moving the rod quickly across the floor in front of the cat to make the 'prey' escape and hide round a corner.

Wait a moment. Most cats will now run over curiously and prepare to spring. Hide the rod under a blanket or a towel – for a cat this will simulate pursuing a mouse in the wild, where small rodents have to be tracked down in their hiding place.

In play, slow activities such as lying in wait and creeping up are alternated with rapid movements. This means the cat doesn't have to rush wildly here and there for minutes on end – as often happens if playing with a laser pointer – which puts quite a strain on the animal. Additionally, when playing with a laser the cat doesn't catch anything, which may lead to problematic behaviour as cats are so

⬇ Playing with your cat is easier than you might think, as long as you pay attention to your pet's mood and interest levels.

success-oriented. There is also a certain risk of injury to the eyes.

Important: quality is always better than quantity. A good toy fishing rod must be robust. What use is the best stimulation and the loveliest game if the fishing rod immediately falls apart? This is both a waste of money and resources and also puts an abrupt end to the fun, which can cause anxiety. Although cats are often tougher and more tolerant in their response to situations than people assume, many are pernickety about certain matters (especially fixed timetables for feeding, playing, stroking and cuddling) and may get upset if the game has to end prematurely.

And finally, don't forget that cats can read your emotions. If the game is no more than a burdensome duty for you, even the most playful cat will cease to enjoy the fun.

Catch one for yourself!

The journey, not the destination, matters. When making things for cats, the intermediate stages that your pets feel, which must be conscientiously investigated, checked and recorded, are as enjoyable as the outcome.

LEATHER CORD FISHING ROD

YOU WILL NEED
- ☐ Ruler
- ☐ Leather cord, approx. 150cm (60in) long
- ☐ Scissors
- ☐ 1 wooden rod or bamboo cane, approx. 50cm (20in) long
- ☐ Cloth tape or heat shrink tubing

TO MAKE
1 Measure, then cut 100cm (40in) of leather cord. Fix the long strip of leather very firmly to the rod or cane with cloth tape or heat shrink tubing.

TIP

Cloth tape is available in various colours and patterns. Heat shrink tubing comes in different colours and sizes (4.8–12 mm) as a set.

2 Measure the remaining leather cord, then cut it into about four equal pieces.
3 To attach these leather pieces to the rod, bundle the strips together, along with the end of the long leather cord, to form a tassel. Tightly secure all the pieces using a strip of cloth tape or heat shrink tubing.

⬇ Leather is irresistible to many cats. Take care that the individual strands are very robust and firmly fixed, so they can't fray or come loose.

➡ A fishing rod designed for cats guarantees fun, a stimulating kind of play and, last but not least, your shared enjoyment of the game!

How did people discover cats?

The story goes that a Roman merchant brought a kitten home from his travels as a present for his wife. The Roman lady was immediately enraptured by the *Cattar* ('mouse catcher', perhaps) and thereafter in the 'eternal city' cats increasingly took the place of the ferrets that had previously been employed to catch mice – probably because cats don't have such a pungent odour and are rather cuddlier.

ROD AND LINE

YOU WILL NEED

- ☐ 1 hose, 15cm (6in) long, 10mm (⅖in) diameter
- ☐ 1 wooden rod or bamboo cane, approx. 50cm (20in) long
- ☐ Cloth tape or heat shrink tubing
- ☐ Elastic cord, approx. 80cm (32in) long, 3mm (⅛in) thick

TO MAKE

1 Push the hose over the rod and fasten the two pieces tightly together with cloth tape or heat shrink tubing.

2 Fasten the elastic cord to the other end of the hose with cloth tape or heat shrink tubing.

3 Slightly fringe the end of the elastic cord to create a lure that's more or less the same size as an insect.

Variation: Pompom bait

YOU WILL NEED

- [ ] Ruler
- [ ] Scissors
- [ ] 1 discarded T-shirt
- [ ] Table fork
- [ ] Elastic cord, approx. 80cm (32in) long, 3mm (⅛in) thick
- [ ] Cloth tape or heat shrink tubing

TO MAKE

1 Measure, then cut strips of T-shirt fabric 0.5–1cm (⅕–²⁄₅in) wide.

2 Knot several strips of fabric together firmly to make a long string. Cut off any superfluous parts. You need an overall length of about 40cm (16in).

3 Wind all the T-shirt string around the fork. Tie a strip of fabric round the middle of the strips and knot it very tightly (see also page 73).

4 Pull everything off the fork and carefully cut open the fabric on either side of the central knot to create a pompom. Leave a longer strip hanging.

5 Attach the longer end of the pompom to the elastic cord with cloth tape or heat shrink tubing. Trim the pompom to the desired size. The smaller it is, the more it will resemble a bumblebee.

← Child's play! The right kind of rod provides hours of play, fun and interest.

Hemingway cats

In the 1930s, a ship's captain presented the American author Ernest Hemingway with a very special animal. The tom cat Snowball had six toes on his forepaws instead of the usual five. This cat was the founding father of the polydactyl Hemingway cat population, which still exists today.

➡ The way you play contributes a great deal to the excitement of the game. Hide the bait so that the cat has to lie in wait for it.

CHINESE FISHING

YOU WILL NEED

☐ Scissors
☐ 1 hair spiral
☐ Cloth tape
☐ 1 chopstick
☐ Elastic cord, 100cm (40in) long, 3mm (⅛in) thick

TO MAKE
1 Cut through the hair spiral once, then use the cloth tape to fasten it to one end to the chopstick.
2 Carefully attach the other end of the spiral to the elastic cord with cloth tape. Please ensure that all of the sharp plastic where you've cut the hair spiral is covered in tape.
3 Tie a tight knot in the cord a little way from the end, then fringe the end.

Dominant paws

American and British scientists have proved that male cats prefer to use their left forepaw to pat toys or prey, whereas females use their right forepaw.

About the author

Heike Grotegut lives in Cologne with her husband, three tom cats and a dog. She studied German language and literature in Paderborn and Cologne and is a trained IT specialist. After several years as a network and systems administrator at one of the Max Planck Institutes in Cologne, she studied animal psychology part-time in Switzerland. A few years ago, she began working as a cat psychologist and in connection with this activity she has been a guest on various media and television broadcasts.

Thanks!

Thank you, dear Bruno, for always making me laugh so much that stress and gloomy thoughts vanish into thin air. What would life be without laughter and humour? Thanks for listening and sometimes for not listening. You are the best.

Of course I thank my cats, who have eagerly contributed to the development, testing and quality control of the ideas in this book. Thanks for the calming purring and cuddling, for fun and games and for always being in a good mood. Paulchen, the dog among the cats, delights me every day with his unwavering cheerfulness. He is the best cat-dog imaginable. One of these days he'll even manage to purr.

Of course, a big thank you must also go to my editor, Kathrin Gutmann, who has taken care of this project with her usual calm and professionalism.

I thank dear Gabi Franz for her wonderful support. I'm so happy that our collaboration has worked so well again. It is always a pleasure to work with her.

Thank you to Janne Reichert for the beautiful photos. She is always my absolutely first choice. I was so pleased that we were able to work together again.

Lastly, I would like to thank all the human and four-footed models for their splendid support. This project would not have been possible without them. It has been so lovely that you have all been involved. Huge praise for the feline models: Cooper and Audrey, Costa, Lucky and Eddy and Rockstar, Krümmel and Löwe, Louis and Missy, Silke and Holly and Toni, the Leverkusen animal shelter (www.tsvlev.de) and along with them Bussi and Kleines and Joker.

Photo credits

Most photos inside the book are by Janne Reichert, Cologne. Additional images are from Shutterstock. The sketches are by Siegfried Lokau, Bochum-Wattenscheid.